MINDSCAPES

Volume 1

Thompson Charlie

An Imprint of Sulis International Press
Los Angeles | London

MINDSCAPES: VOLUME 1
Copyright ©2020 by Thompson Charlie. All rights reserved.

Cover picture by Photo by Luiz Felipe.
Cover design by Cassandra Anderson.

Except for brief quotations for reviews, no part of this book may be reproduced in any form or by any electronic or mechanical means, including information storage and retrieval systems, without written permission from the publisher.
Email: info@sulisinternational.com.

Library of Congress Control Number: 2020905947
ISBN (print): 978-1-946849-72-4
ISBN (eBook): 978-1-946849-73-1

Published by Sulis Press
An Imprint of Sulis International
Los Angeles | London

www.sulisinternational.com

Dedication

to loved ones left in haste
alone to pine in wretched waste
their lives rapt in torn drapes

all those who left the land
to risk their lives in quest of change
till they returned as strangers

and all who lost their lives
in quest of a just and loving society
where every man thrives

you peel yourself in the mirror
broken! lost! battered!
then in your mangled heart
explodes a maze of razor wire
a burning mind's fluid fire
the MINDSCAPES

Contents

Consciousness 1
Blessings 3
How I Died on the Street 5
Days of the Tyrant 7
Silver Jubilee 9
Born of Terror 11
Momentary Thought 13
Bubble 15
Beware 17
The Cynic 19
Mindscapes 21
In My Room 23
My Identity 25
Lost Dawn 27
My Nights 28
Election 2018 30
Murambatsvina Mayhem 32
Why did they Die? 34
Looking Back 36
The Hararean Exile 38
Lamentation of the Citizen 40
My Afrika 43
It is not a S**t Hole 45
Childless Widower 47
I Am Sorry 49
The Call of Tradition 51
Cardboard People 1 53
Acceptance 55
Silence 57
The Suicide 59
Song of an Absent Father 61
Promise Forever 62
Jolted 64
In the End 66
About You 68
Love Not Fear 70
Why Do I Write? 72
Wake Child Go 74
I Who Could Not See 76
The True Chimurenga 77
Chaos 78
God Save 79
Cardboard People 2 81
Truth be Handled 83
On the Precipice 85
Gestapo Son 87
Cornered 89
Post Elections 2018 91

Military Junta	93
None but Ourselves	95
Without You	97
Agony	99
Salvation	101
Colour Blind	103
Throne of Freedom	105
Waiting in Vain	107
Dauntless	109
When Nothing Turns	111
Our Burning Hunger	113
About the Publisher	115

Consciousness

when a man loses the light of his mind
his blighted soul darkens
and turns into a devil's playground

when a man loses his purpose in life
he loses the sail of his ship
and there can be nothing worse

but when he takes charge of his past
and the things he robbed himself
he becomes a calm sea for the ship of life

Blessings

all thoughts of anxiety
rage sadness and worry
only create noise in my head
there is nothing more i can do
than open space for God's bidding
his blessings the void to fill

his blessings received
are best used in the service of others
for only given to the benefit of others
shall blessings bring rewards
work wait give with honour
and connect with your best

How I Died on the Street

i went out not knowing what i had
abused by worry i tortured my mind
till i learned to trust in new attitude
to go out without thought or worry
to give my life to God's plan
mine only to know i was the story

light of heart i went out
to meet the day and work with it
never wishing it were not on me
only knowing mine was mine
to die to reactive thought and feeling
to find purpose in adversity

i went out without knowing
whether it was better to live or die
embracing the flow and dying to pain
i perched on wooden pole benches
washing away my past in loneliness
i walked life, life walking me

Days of the Tyrant

we will remember ever after
the hideous murders and craft
blitz on our common liberties
and trodden dignity

incessant we shall pray
that in the stir of new day
we may not in our hearts cease
the bellows that stoke our dreams

and fearless we will fight
until the vampire espies in his skull
our pitchforks doomed to skit
his curse in history's acid

Silver Jubilee

showers of shame
spew from barren clouds
hunger falling like a shroud

foolish dark hearts
grasping their filthy loot
hail the despot

weeping and abhorred
the poor stumble
voiceless they tumble

and the daughters
in anguish wriggle
under militia rape

wheels stop turning
in mud of rust they soak
choking in the vast silence
of derelict manufacture

into voids we descend
pranks of victory on crippled farms
barely whitewash our minds

victuals unwholesome
empty plates and cups
grace our tables

speechless zombies
bereft of motion and passion
we peep into our graves

Born of Terror

his reign subsists on chaos
murder rape and sleaze
amassing alps of wealth
gauchely he struts on stage
and frostily storms on virtue
emblazoning his evil symmetry
without rue but mulish pride
he severs all value asunder
snipes madly like a ruffian
holing our begotten evolution
but terror hardens the children
his flames bake their anger
behold them make the charge
sons of boiling blood
dauntless their lives they wager
like the rats every cat admires
a finer future their eyes glitter

than stolen jewels of *marange*[1]
and their timbre of voice imbued
with offended energy nameless
smothers the vampire's songs
the offended potency
of the spirits in the mists

---

[1] Marange: Diamonds were discovered in this place in Zimbabwe. $15 Billion worth of diamonds went missing, allegedly misused by the president.

Momentary Thought

oh Lord
why man is flint of heart

brutal and wanton in pursuit
of callous and foul exploit

why his mind exalts
in the deception of cults

why cemetery minds delight
whenever death is an obvious stain

why arrogance crouches on the fringe
of all peace that makes a bridge

why much sin in white clothes
adorn the flock making the hordes

Bubble

stitched in controversy
putrid abrogation
and eclipsed love
i swell in agony

lonely
dying
alive

rising in my secret
in the values of my heart
futility of venal reign
syphoned is my agony

loving
living
bubbling

ecstasy

o the soft kiss of new life
wrapped in maiden loins
my heart in the hide of a lion
slumber-less i roam the world

Beware

even when reign
on diabolic wings fly
in tar most evil soak
and peace wantonly strike
be still at the shrine
of respect divine

but even you
evil who sold soul
heart shut to reason
and dredged up past season
the abominable to justify
murder maim and abuse
the bill for you looms

o brother i loved you
walked we together once
but i hate the evil you became
now lost in your insolent glory
you who sops in ecstasy
of crimes against humanity
and blasphemy of the sacred

your blow struck
jolting me into chambers
where the bottomless cries
jam tortured throats
of frosty hungry orphans
laving in torrential grief

of pleas suing riposte

steeped in your pillage
you roll your baleful eyes
in lust scratch your crotch
oblivious the mess you adore
for the bull's eye our spear flies
to slay in glory eternal

The Cynic

now i see
it was no revolt
born against
the trite wisdom
of our elders

oh it was
not an assault
upon the
common trust
of our custom

it was
an open assault
upon the
common habit
of our failure

Mindscapes

the eye peeled wisdom
footprints skirting death
ignited streaks of a broken life
trussed in shattered birth-rights
anaesthetized with propaganda

the path coiled in giddiness
reciting a fact in silent uproar
rupturing the skin of darkness
dread and grafted rage
of dreams cudgelled by oppression

in shattering wilds alienating
i collided with darkness and day
minding not what the hand held to eat
over the night I rested my weary soul
the satirizing breath of wise owls
cushioning my cardboard mattress
where tawny ribs sketched my misery
the core of my life steeped in ignominy
i became jetsam of the revolution

the gun that grazed my temple
the fists, the kicks, the stabs
and the punitive fire of my failures
melted in the barrel of my pen
into stubborn life that would not die
flesh that escaped from a pie
to feed the tyrant's lie

stinking like un-wiped bottoms
the eyeless sockets of murdered babies
was a shame upon my muteness

then the frugal peace of my silence
poured out a river of vitriol
the gore of chopped bodies shimmering
in a wraith of prophetic mist

giant beetles of steel
purred and farted
on black ribbons
belching insults
into my lungs
squealing my life
my life without me

tripping upon my shadow
the mindscapes exploded
scattering
my ruptured humanity

now by the blood-river
where rent garments lie tossed
in the lap of blazing hope
my path specked with stardust
and the wilderness I walked a wonder
bruised, battered, mangled
i am reborn of martyred blood

In My Room

each day i wake up
the sunlight tasselling my world
its soft myriad fingers
prod to life the curtain on my window
a flower bursting luscious lips
beauty validated in isolation
as honest work purified in sweat
deeper into the latent secret bowls
of the infinite surge of promises
is reflected my dead past
awake asleep or perhaps dead
my new life spans
into a myriad worlds

My Identity

i am the fractured energy
in the synergies of life

i move on two legs
lanced by the evil that slits
covenants of human grace
o look at me and see
the anger of my children

i breathe hot air
coiled in spirals of despair
and let out those songs
the oppressor burns alive
yes i walk in broken shoes
of those who lost toes
and no longer grieve

the print of my finger
is a net, a labyrinth maze
of untold captured stories
wasted fate and bludgeoned hopes
burned corpses and blood drops
gulped in tyrannical madness

i am stamped
with the blood of humanity
trampled, loved, abhorred
a son of the motherland
the face of covered histories
blazing in the mud-plain

Lost Dawn

pain forks into my heart
and as i dig nose in the tarmac
i spy how your teeth fell
splitting under steely blows
of anvil-blind cruelty

i turn with guilt
dust peeling off the pestilence
that socked our men into exile
the virus of our silence
a mantle of darkness

son bring me my spear
for the evil one takes pride
in skinning our clan
brother pick up your shield
the tick sues our blood

My Nights

i spend sleepless nights
my happiness flying away
rapt in the wilderness
my soul swabs in sadness
and bobs in suds of futility
my body, like a derelict path
pines for the velvet prints
dense soft velvet prints
impressed by my children
and my throat rips burning
for the love of my wife
longing for the reunion
to us that must come
when the despot goes

Election 2018

sights dim with blood
of citizens struck to death
in the satanic love of power
by time's barbaric robbers

minds stand still
in remembrance of those slain
hunted, tortured and exiled
for stumbling upon their voice

bodies girdle sack-cloth
deprived of peace everywhere
dying, condemned, journeying
into tombs of hate

Murambatsvina[2] Mayhem

we broke sleep at dawn
garbed in merry sacrifice
winter bound not our limbs
and basking in our creative glory
change murmured an amazing story
cast out of the sludge of paucity

what distances had we toiled through
what shade of darkness and absence!
until the blood of our might
against it trod a spiteful shock
as horrid as the dictator's heart
so hideous our eyes ever saw

such odium never soiled the soul
such darkness never swept the land
that grey like bees we rose
skirting rubbish piles leaping on the outskirts
we beat the sullied neglect of ages
charged with the thrill of un-caged power
our gifts and talents wound in laughter
switched on were our livelihood bulbs
mending our brokenness after the war
THE PEOPLE'S WAR

---

[2] On July 16 2005, in the middle of winter, a political initiative (operation clear the filth) hiding behind restoring order, largely viewed by opposition and political analysts as punishing the people for not voting for the ruling party, was launched in Zimbabwe.

then baying and coughing a sinister roll
ghastly caterpillars quaked the land
clawing down all brick and mortar
trampling glass, wood, metal, livelihoods
into lurid heaps of smoking grief

awed, pacing by the lewd rubble
a piteous sight nearly struck me blind
for blood soaked out of the debris
bereft of life a tiny hand clawed out
i mopped tears off my cheeks
for the arm that wanted to live
with a body buried alive;
then a shrieking voice ripped the air
as a woman's womb untimely released

so the weird mist retreated in bloody shame
its shadow captured in the cold vacant stare
of yet another heart attack victim
and when the grieving morning swelled
again hypothermia had rung the sullen bell -
silence for another gran had departed

all these hearts the dictator despised
humiliated, tortured and dispatched
all these souls that never lifted a hand
as their humanity was cast into trash
do they sleep and rest in peace?

Why did they Die?

i speak to myself all the time
the path of loneliness beckoning
into the echo of their moans
a blaze stoked by misty voices
awash with butterfly souls

the track a puss-yellow opened
spilling both truth and lies
into where naked bodies lie
internalising our common failure
to skin time's greatest lie

the seat a bubbling foam
the room leapt into a storm
detonating a molten turbulence
of desires trapped in lame promises
bleached out in pools of denial

i speak to myself sometimes
at knife-point of painful accusations
cutting into spine of catharsis
my rights emasculated in the glory
of a frankenstein horror

the lie trips around its wit
and cowards quit
but i refuse to be quiet
beaten up to salt

i am inspired that
their seed is gold

bold

behold

aaaaahhhh
r-e-v-o-l-u-t-i-o-n!

Looking Back

pot-holes yawn
a toothless grin into the future
burning the green lawn
where I rolled my hauteur

tearful regrets
abrade peace of mind
exposing all the secrets
once my joyous find

i gaze behind
combing the wrong turn
where lost i the way
into the demon's lair

i see with shrouded eyes
the jagged boulder i lifted
slip through my grasp
to peel my naked toes

with cantankerous pain
of an emotional prodigal
who gambled in false glory
myself i skin my world

i stand alone
alone against the world
whose poisoned nectar i sucked
a world i thought was gold

a cry rings
and death sings
wrapped in veils of fear
i float on strange barge

yes i float on
away from my children
yes i float away
on mud like gold

The Hararean Exile

fly out like a butterfly
spin petals of vast truth
the kind to grace the land

into lands tragic to others
walk and love the earth
let dust caking your weary feet
be the icing of ageless wisdom

cross the river of grace-lands
harare's flood of hegemony and hate
rise above spirals of broken hearts
like an eagle come out of hades
knowing one day you will return
a man intimately reborn

let no mountain before you rise
i broke the fat border patrol voice
with the roar of my fiery poetry
echoes of what was human
converging in what was rare
the intimacy of experience
and the bare unsparing shock
exploding in a burning cloak

purchase not the tragedies of history
sold in the pawnshop of obituaries
quake not the bubble-gum fangs
of the faithless serpents

for the world awaits to give
to those who never tire

go seek and love
gather up your self-hood go
and write what none ever saw

Lamentation of the Citizen

what shall i say when i remained quiet
whilst they took my neighbour away?
his children's faces bleached with tears
and their marrow gnawed by fangs of sorrow
i who kept my silence
what will i say?

that i saw them coming
rapt in darkness with cruel stride
to steal his life and only land?
how could i not be touched?
when next would be my wealth
my life, my land

our thin lives puppets on a stage
future a writhing shadow on the wall
they sought to erase our humanity
our names into graves of non-history
corrupting children to slay their fathers
rape, spy on mothers, brothers and sisters

in our torn faded clothes
we fought the noose over our bleak destiny
with death yapping at our heals
our feet trudged on to alien lands
our souls hungry at the altar of justice
we jostled for left overs in exile

scattered all over alien lands

our words ring hollow like dead voices
our wives and children not understanding
men who flee their homesteads
their hope waning on the back of prayers
holding onto things already lost

their horrors pursue me
echoing everywhere in the silence and noise
whipping, kicking, stabbing, interrogating
i limp and parry an ignominious death
choking down screams in my throat
i die a thousand deaths on the street

i see my kinsmen with hollow faces
their eyes deathly marbles rolling wildly
bob in fiery sockets of skinny heads
their knees thicker than their shrunken thighs
the tarmac they walk an endless ribbon
of misery, rage, turmoil and torture

the tyrant wants me to see through his eyes
to praise my freedom in his slavery
and spread the gospel of his longing
i who will not serve against the truth
the sun shines on his deeds, the wind speaks
for the world to see, its ears to hear

i see them all, i hear them all
the women their vile organs raped
the sons whose limbs they tore apart
jailed, kidnapped, and murdered
their groans, their cries, their supplications
walk with me till judgement day

what shall i say now that i speak?
you who has torn the roof off our houses
desecrated the freedom fighter's tomb
and erased piety from your glossary
you whose waste of hatred purifies us
in your fetid power is the seed of freedom

i who now will forever speak
i who walks in the martyrs' blood
looking for the shield of justice you stole
the blighted chapters of our constitution
my mind the reality of a scary prize
i lay down my life for peace

My Afrika

there is more nothing my own
than the freedom of my heart
the pulse that searches
the wilderness for the tame
till the cold wide sea
i am forced to stand in awe
the sun of *afrika* all over me
shining like a fire of gold
smiles of warm souls
warriors and pretty daughters
from cape to *cairo*
afrika your enchanting beauty
stirs my pride

It is not a S**t Hole

i who came out of what was left
from the beauty of origins
blooming fire of the flame lily
soft wisp of the natal-red-top
spec in scattered confusion
of colonial configuration
i dance into a new arena
of the drum that thunders
for peaceful slumber of the spirits
purged by the spite of history
a new dance telling the story
how we moved into what is
the spiritual death of the ego
out of the conceit and bigotry
ensnaring dear presidents
who have forgotten *afrika*
is the cradle of humankind
obliterating its benevolence
by tweeting in their insolence
that it is a s**t-hole

Childless Widower

i see
you are heavy
you stand the world
leaning on grief

loneliness chokes
your joy in the marrow
shattering portraits
of pending morrows

every day
you watch the sun
the agony siphoning
away your breath

every night
you sit the darkness
the rustle of her dress
choked in silence

I Am Sorry

in that room
where our love grew
i will come to sew
what is torn

please
do not make me cry
when my hand seeks
to mend the seam
that crowns our love

you say
i get lost in mess
but wars lost
and abuse of the land
are hateful to my spirit

i will
oh i will return
to your sweet sun
to the heat
warming my space

The Call of Tradition

we have buried our dead
their graves crammed on anthills
the silent festivals of the earth
lie unsung in the songs of slaves

the *jikinya* dance along the memory
has captured the heart of Mwango
in ecstasy he lies
driven to the purity of tradition
and the drum thunders his resolution

naked we have buried them all
suppose they all heard ancestor- calls
hanging from a cold and sooty nose
now the leaping mediums vanish naked
and we listen to the heart-beat of Mwango
but alas driven to the purity of tradition
dig another grave
in the triumph of another resolution

Cardboard People 1

all is quiet
the world sleeps
but the cardboard people
teeth heavy with tartar
defy their exhaustion
all the shear pain
of a self-abusive pace
pushing and shoving
a trolley atlas laden
with heaps of white paper
and cardboard box
in the haze of dawn
unkindly spared
by ice-cold swords
a corpse they skirt around
scarves girdling necks
bodies roughly draped
in black sooty garbs
the sweat of many days
caked on itchy skin
on their weird forms
backpack wardrobes mounted
they slice through the mist
under dim eyes of lights
wheels of their trolleys
in a throttled murmur
hum through the silence
their day has begun
on light tennis shoes

cardboard plugging holes
that smile in the soles
their journey dauntless
a million steps foraging
into desolate tidings
the snarl of xenophobia
stalking behind

Acceptance

take him that the lord gave
and walk your soul into his shoes
take her that the lord gave
and walk your soul into her shoes
turn not the leaves on the ground
but pick the ripest of fruits
growing on the tree you grafted
travel the distance from loneliness
and ride your trip rapt in comeliness
for you have elected your journey
on the horse of tolerance
go into the world clothed in joy
and never let it slip away
for it is the way you should go
lace your heart with fair ribbon
for the one you have chosen
and crave not for things impossible
things strewn out of choice
or yonder the realms of your bliss
for the sanctity of your marriage
bears no substitute but bitterness
tears and tattered hearts
that may never mend in divorce

Silence

the judge awaits at hague
his gavel locked in mid-air
on the stairs the old man leans
spitting his horror away

wombs untimely ripped
dripping blood of torn foetus
the staring eye-sockets
roasted flesh on plastic fire
melted bodies lost in acid
and pouring gore from limbs amputated
shower on the brood
stains that will never fade

truth
       exhausts
              her
                      patience
and the court-room sits in silence
listening to the rage in the docket
spilling all over the silence

silence
       judging
              silence

interrogating *sadc* [3]

---

[3] Southern African Development Community.

interrogating africa union
interrogating united nations
interrogating our systems

truth
       exhausts
              her
                      patience!

The Suicide

i see escape
an end setting me free
in telephonic wires
that kiss my neck

i am the seeker
who lost sight
the doomed guide
who cannot pick
the spoor

this wire
on my neck
the only that cared
my pants soiled
with the shit promise
of a false dream

i have lost
all i had
my heart
my mind
my soul

i had stolen
that which gave
place amongst you
in darkness and turmoil
this heavy laden world
i quit, you face . . .

Song of an Absent Father

i have journeyed lands afar
to patch our lame future
yes my back is sore
yet it swells upon my heart
to nurture your able spirits
oh it bursts upon my sad soul
to sate your hungry vessels
to celebrate your lives
and link your worlds

i have journeyed lands afar
to fetch that sunshine
whipped out of our lives
i will fly back to you love
a charged parcel of abundance
all promise made eternal
yes I will fly back my love
with the wonder of the wilderness
and all you missed

Promise Forever

i will be full of life
secreting that love
daubed with faith
        and ardour

o! my love
you are all I live for
all riches I desire
        in this world

when I am away
and I cannot hold you
all the time pining away
in the sucking fury of your absence
        i cannot wait

o! sweetheart
i thrive in your space
the cold sun in my heart
for ever charged
        with ecstasy

Jolted

i felt in my heart drizzle
dew on pages of terror
a purity that revives all broken
to live up not on their knees
but walk their souls fearless
without end to purpose

lonely in Joburg
silence boiling over
my blood food for bugs
turning scabby and falling
into the latrine of howling
scowling surly poverty
like a prisoner of war
gazing through a chink
i saw in one wink
my life tearing apart
crumble into a dark heap
deep into the sadistic deep
my children unable to fathom
me their lost father

my spirit defiant
the python that never died
born of a tribe inured to terror
with busted skin and laughter
i trickled out of the gutter
where dejection slaughtered
the thin gift of sanity

my eye peered
into misted depths of sorrow
razed fields and barren fallows
of sham ideas devised
sinking without end
where men drop their souls
and become worthless jokes

my hand on the plough
now my bitten lip bleeds
to water the seeds
that alone must be watered
by the blood of martyrs
and our spitting saliva

In the End

the one who is not there
will come
the one who is missing
one day will be there

the one who left in agony
and abject loneliness
to dance hell's wild orchestra
his ragged life spat in the gutter
one who licked his lips for supper
and survived the biblical demons
one day will return
his skin of milk reborn

the one who is not there
the one rapt in wilderness
and pages of a lost odyssey
will stride out of the murk

About You

i have rediscovered my name
in the tremor of your breast
the warm faith of your love
mystifies the wine of my tent
the print on my blood-scroll
evolves on the seed of your soul
and i know you soar in the sky
for my spirit to seek
but so long my long love
i have discovered my copious share
in the star all people stare
despite haunting pain of separation
songs nudge reach and meet
so the gentle breath of your sleep
caresses the restlessness in my heart
and the dimpled cheeks in the rhythm
of passion-caged memories
exalt our pining rose bed

Love Not Fear

the undercurrent stirs alive
bathing in petals of light
a tower-light after the rude awakening
from a shamed rude conscience
i blaze out of the darkness
and the hunger in my mind
melting the chains of self-remand
celebrates suffered losses
as i tread beyond their measure
my enemies toothless all tumble
to a power beyond peace
my poverty peeling off
like a boogie nightmare wrecks to dust
drying up the sulphurous ignominy
my love bursts, overflows and heals
the pain of tears shed for loved ones
cleaning the scars of my life
now wars i sought to win in vain
flop before my iron resolve
and from atop the cliff of losses
once more i leap into the arena
my pen a flaming sword of ink
rip flesh and bone for new world
a world forever to hold

Why Do I Write?

i saw light
and all was good
all bright and hanging on vision
words flourishing in my growth
spreading butter on crusty mind
melting the dust of ignorance
and wisdom roused from slumber
to search my conscience
hungry to hold the grail

then all became silent
steeled in silence and abuse
and between my feet was a bomb
blasting me into the air
where birth and birth-right
were torn to meaningless shreds
where the palm of fate
was filled with boiling blood
of tortured cynical psyches
and messed up nerves

crumpled like cigarette
the smell of my burning wounds
spiralled in livid questions
what self am I?
do I wake or dream?
or do I die alive?
my being crumbling
who then to my redemption hurtles?

another cloud ruptured
and the fire my back swallowed
scraped through my mouth
the stark revelations
flaming out the horrific stories
yelled for therapeutic healing
and tons of swallowed silence
tied my heart to humanity

Wake Child Go

the way is too long
go meet the pregnant world
and her secrets learn
gone are all the guides
and orphans all crouch
ready to abandon
the homesteads diseased

a drum in the tannery lies
taut with leaping rhythms
and lessons to be learned
yourself initiate orphan
deeds mighty in blood hide
let in your hand breathe
their beauty

go child go
death spares no one
when our sweet ones go
slumber not in prayer
rest not in search
wake child go
meet the pregnant world

I Who Could Not See

pure joy of an ex-future dream
a seed from two broken hearts
i who passed to batten your joy
my footsteps sterilized in truth
will pace the eyelids of your sleep

i flesh of fury
turned so by your evil hands
in my blood boils the judgement
only packaged for you who spit venom
to blight all sacred creation

i who screamed in silence
my cry echoing in my mother's voice
that your shameless hands recoil
from brutally shredding her womb
will be waiting in your tomb

The True *Chimurenga*

the true *chimurenga*[4]
stands up
for the oppressed
and against reprise

the true *chimurenga*
is forward looking
embraces change
and denies obscurity
of a people's future

the true *chimurenga*
beckons the nation
to humane renaissance
building paradigms
for the morrow

the true *chimurenga*
is a fine tableau
of snug gifts shared
in reconciliation

---

[4] *Chimurenga*: Shona word for revolution.

Chaos

i stare towards the ground
at the hunger-dislocated shadow
the flesh of human ideals
dignity and moral obligations
peel off the bones
washing in alkaloid illusions
of political saliva

i wade into the past
through the corridor of oppression
unfinished concepts in court chambers
cold unopened secret pages
and gagged up voices
victims before and after injustice
bleed wounds of million histories

i grope into the future
through mists of unending tunnel
neurotic flaunt of gyrating whores
weeping hearts and alienated souls
trapped in philosophic waves
and the trauma of persecution
i meet loss of humanization

God Save

jagged-bank rivers
of acute broken glass
flow through my heart

the ulcers open
laved in ripping pain
they wash in anger

i open the door
you only entered
and meet my pain

i become angry
why in that hurry
you were dispatched

i am still wretched
about my failure
to save your life
and i plead with God
to save one woman so good
from pain so rude

Cardboard People 2

combing through dark hope
all swirl in a quaking wind
cruel as a wicked bride
the dance shivers into the future
bonnet and apron torn to shreds.
blood spilled from countless wombs
of wives and concubine dreams
crown a field of broken promises,
all expectation falling apart
in a clumsy impotent rage.
the letters crash upon my chest
thick, heavy, long and short,
a writhing mass of slippery worms
coiling on voices of martyred lives,
they urge my tortured outlet
to record syllables of broken soles
and the screaming sweat of outcast souls
carrying cardboard to the scrap-yard
they yell the rage of exiles
comesa[5] like a starved whore
dances in lecherous *sadc*[6] mirror
their faces to the lying moon turned
they cover faeces with red rose petals
as un[7] stands snout in the clouds
and au[8] lost in cigarette smoke

---

[5] Common Market for Eastern and Southern Africa.
[6] Southern African Development Community.
[7] United Nations.
[8] African Union.

the sane wail in disbelief
at afrika's tragic circus
i stand beside broken statues
swallowing the cataclysmic pulse
of lost tracks and grubby lives
torn and tossed day to day
away in bins of cold neglect
to rot and freeze in *joburg* winter.
disaster sprouts around the high court
with broken trees yelling their plight;
why turn your eyes to the sky;
do you fear to espy the truth
mirrored in the guttered *lazarus*
whose tawny hungry boot-swept ribs
press the pavement in the night?
your roses grafted on wilting hearts
plastic smiles and tales of plenty
coat alive a famished corpse.

Truth be Handled

the blind feeling erupts
against the muscle of its prison
bursting the lids of its bated sight
it mutates in cotyledons of sin
the sin of a murdering regime

they raised a gun to my lip
that i should not expose their sin
but i saw my silence was the bigger sin
like the cholera in the puddles
waiting to claim us all

now each day the faces grow long
battening the tyrant's appetite
the struggle, the spirits, everything
captured in heaven's white light
sigh a glorious bloom on the retina

yes our journey whips on
a story told by parched tongues
scorched, peeled, cheeky
it writhes like a skinless worm
destiny and soul immortal

we kneel at the altar of victory
peace the epiphany of our struggle
will grace the finger of our life
broken bones and roasted flesh
torn wombs and rivers of blood

On the Precipice

i totter on wobbly feet
dancing weirdly on the edge
mesmerized by dizzying spaces
and the pernicious distances
that waft around the obscene
horrors of my broken corpse
the shards of a tragic end?

                    gyrating screams
              splitting eardrums
        rupturing the tiny breasts
and the halo of my children's life

shame
     pain
          awakening
                              pain

the chafed spirit wakes
ripping shafts tear into my sorrow
in the agony of exile and displacement
i roast over fires of truth
all the fears
and the tears
mangled in a spineless mess
of worthless currency

Gestapo Son

son you shame us
you inherit strange tactics
murderers of your people
used to silence reason

children cry
sounds of breaking bones
and blood spilled in plunder
feed the people's anger

son oh what shame
why police and soldier
bathing in people's blood
for madness not ours?

Cornered

i open the mass graves of martyrs
my eyes piercing the gory mist
burn the despot naked of all lies
that bury our vanishing heroes;
radical tears filter me of all fears
as i parry the crocodile threats
sired of wild fascist lunatic minds
i nail silence into a coffin
and they nail me into exile
ME and MY RIGHTS

Post Elections 2018

i feel a bomb
a bomb under the people's skull
their eyes spilling rivers of pain
chafed by the dust of deceit
hoofed up by political cohorts
fooling the sons of afrika

i see fooled limbs gathering
waste of departed peace
and the coming ambivalent dawn
bloodied with deceit
an army that salutes not
a president who a gun never fired

i hear tons of elegiac voices
trooping across the sky
in cynical boots of reason
questioning the dismal season
why assign the vampire
to heal the wounds it gave?

Military Junta

they ride
the caravan of evil
the scourge of hell
ripping out flesh
from the people's back

despotic snipers
they relegate citizens
to trespassers and tramps
marginal exiles
and illegal settlers

coup plotters
they declare themselves
God's anointed kings
by merit of war
to rule forever

they bare teeth
obscenely scornful
to defend their plunder
and wanton rape
of the nation

None but Ourselves

time collapses on the dreams
and flung in gory abyss
a nation at ransom burns
silvering hairs in foreign lands
has become our acceptance
naked witches of deceit
celebrate deceitful unity
stupid fountains of diesel
bleak harvests and mass murder
blighting a beautiful land
as the sun goes up
who will clean up clean
the inferno of horrors
spewed by a pitiless regime?
the lawless *green bombers*[9]
and the murdering militia
who will make them plead

for *Gukurahundi*?
and those they stole upon
the children who were never seen
who will give them justice?
and what they did with them?
who will......?

---

[9] *Green bombers*: name synonymous with green flies used by people to call ruling party youth trained to terrorise all party opposition. Shortly after independence in 1980, thousands of people were massacred by the Zimbabwean army in the Matabeleland Province.

Without You

each day
i open my eyes
your picture glitters
all drenched in dew

i listen
sorely without end
always up the tree
listening for your laughter

the wind
becomes quiet
and my eyes strain
for you in vain

i forget
to take my meals
without you
i am dying

Agony

you sleep alone
the slight rest beneath the sheets
split in whipping silence

i sleep under the sky
the cold church concrete
cuddling the love i secrete

still morning comes
your pain approaches in the wind
and i espy your wounded heart

my sad lonely children
peer at me in sick dreams
their pain licking my heart

hopes touch my soul
and their toil digging into my heart
is a blow staggering my peace

tears fall on the page
where despair crawls in a rage
i refuse to die in that cage

heart in mist
i grope around
lost, broken
shattered!

Salvation

filtering like crap
through sludge of abusive borders
they whirled in the cesspool
dazed, rootless and confused
the jetsam of political fiasco

then picking up
in scrapyards of redemption
tapping echoes stuck in dry corridors
of freedom's empty river-bed
they swallowed the horrors

        waking
surfacing   rising

telling a pyramid story
of man chasing after wind-bags
vast riches of cruelty begotten
yet none ever used interred

Colour Blind

i call you no name
that takes away your fame
i kiss your lips, all your form
with peace and love that never changes
and you will strip yourself naked
that I should look at your body
still I will look in your eyes, your face
but I will see no difference

Throne of Freedom

if we could untie the reigns
cast away the racial stirrups
and unlearn the lies of dogma
what darkness will rise against
the piercing light?

if i could stop in stride
softly, softly grasp your hand
drunk with love like a bride
would you embrace my mortality
and purify my tainted soul?

if i could kneel
humbly kneel upon my pride
my heart to beg your heart
and swim across the divide
would you cross the past?

Waiting in Vain

to strange music we dance
like mice we frown and glance
and timid, we shiver down the heath
in denial of our own death

we tip cactus to quench our thirst
and in our sad silence assert:
'better in poverty our glory be
than suffer the blood of insurrection'

no more birds flirt in the sky
like a derelict city in a cursed dream
our ghost-eyes cast a cynical beam
our burden to wait for Jesus

Dauntless

through crevices of hope
our broken eyes grope
the path out of nowhere
a free-way of political rage
challenging history's page

stalwart we fare forward
never looking backward
with charity for our enemies
riding on love born of remedies
and wisdom dug of tragedies

stalwart we fare forward
to our loved ones homeward
we will return by will
thriving in rainbow glory
of a story above their story

When Nothing Turns

at the heart of our dread
where lost our knees buckle
at the still point of the struggle
only there lies the rich land
for the seed of change to plant
only there stands the shrine
the nation's curse to burn

Our Burning Hunger

we have said
all things sad
but their lips have not spoken
to mend what is broken

we have not lived
we have not seen
oh how we all have dearly loved
to be where we could have been

If you enjoyed this book, please consider leaving an online review. The author would appreciate reading your thoughts.

About the author

Thompson Charlie is a former school teacher turned poet, writer and counsellor. He has published some of his poetry works online with Poetry Potion and Munyori. His debut novel, *Shattered 1: The impact*, was published in 2020 by Sulis International Press under their imprint of Riversong Books.

Thompson Charlie lives in exile in Johannesburg, South Africa where he spends most of his time travelling, doing charity work with local and foreign unaccompanied minors, orphans and youth at risk. He also does voluntary counselling for LifeLine Johannesburg, a non-governmental organization based in Johannesburg.

Thompson Charlie is happily married to Margaret and they have been blessed with three sons.

When he has taken care of serious business, Thompson either sneaks into his magical world of poetical reveries with good music that shakes the body or just loses his mind to nature and appreciating the beauty of feeling alive in the universe.

About the Publisher

Sulis International Press publishes select fiction and nonfiction in a variety of genres under four imprints: Riversong Books, Sulis Academic Press, Sulis Press, and Keledei Publications.

For more, visit the website at
https://sulisinternational.com

Subscribe to the newsletter at
https://sulisinternational.com/subscribe/

Follow on social media
https://www.facebook.com/SulisInternational
https://twitter.com/Sulis_Intl
https://www.pinterest.com/Sulis_Intl/
https://www.instagram.com/sulis_international/

www.ingramcontent.com/pod-product-compliance
Lightning Source LLC
Chambersburg PA
CBHW030155100526
44592CB00009B/284